I
CAN'T
FORGET
THE
BOMB

*Barefoot Gen
and the
Atomic Bombing
of Hiroshima:
A Memoir*

KEIJI
NAKAZAWA

LAST GASP

I CAN'T FORGET THE BOMB

Barefoot Gen and the Atomic Bombing of Hiroshima: A Memoir

Story and art
KEIJI NAKAZAWA

Translation
NOBUTOSHI KOHARA

Additional Translation
AJANI OLOYE

Editor
RICHARD MINEAR

Cover & book design, lettering
EVAN HAYDEN

Production
COLIN TURNER

Publisher
RONALD E. TURNER

Published by
LAST GASP OF SAN FRANCISCO
777 Florida Street, San Francisco, California, 94110
www.lastgasp.com

ISBN: 978-0-86719-896-6

First Printing, 2023

Printed in China

I
CAN'T
FORGET
THE
BOMB

1. FATHER OPPOSED THE WAR

The Atomic Bomb Dome sits at the center of Hiroshima. Less than a mile away is Funairi Hommachi. That's where I was born and raised. I remember clearly the period 1944-1945, the final stage of the Pacific War.

We were a family of seven. To be more accurate, we were a family of eight: my mother was carrying a baby due in August.

Father—quite eccentric—had many interests. For generations, lacquering wooden clogs had been the Nakazawa family business. However, that wasn't enough for Father, and when he was young he went to Kyoto to learn how to do gold-relief lacquer and Japanese ink painting. So he was a Japanese ink painter and a gold-relief lacquer artist. What's more, he participated in theater and joined a leftist theater group in Hiroshima. At that time, its repertory included Maxim Gorky's *The Lower Depths* and Shimazaki Tōson's *Before the Dawn*. Because they staged radical plays, the group was raided frequently by the Thought Police, was under constant surveillance, and was infiltrated by police spies. A commemorative photo of the members of the group served as irrefutable proof, and they were all arrested as thought criminals and thrown into Hiroshima jail.

After Father disappeared, I asked Mother, "What's happened to Father?" But she hid the truth from us: "He's gone to take his physical for the military." I met a survivor of the theater group recently and learned about that time, and at last I was able to bring my fragmentary memories into focus.

I can't forget Father's homecoming after his release from six months in Hiroshima jail. He was hunched over and frequently touched his teeth. They were all loose. Human beings are active when they have enough salt in their diet. So in jail the authorities removed salt from the diet. Deprived of salt, the body's joints stop functioning. He was tortured, too. Father's teeth grew loose, and his muscles atrophied. He couldn't hold a rice bowl; if he tried, he dropped it. His sad condition is seared onto my retinas.

Whenever we sat around the low table at mealtimes, Father forced us kids to sit up straight, legs crossed under us. And he would lecture us. Father told us, "Japan is absolutely going to lose this war. This war of aggression is wrong." And he'd add: "We'll be defeated. Any day now, we'll lose. But by the time you've grown up, good times will come when you'll be able to eat your fill: noodles, bread, white rice."

In 1944 and 1945, there was real starvation in Hiroshima. There was nothing to eat—even the vines of sweet potato plants were a luxury. We made dumplings from the dregs of soybeans, by pulverizing dried up sweet potatoes, and from sorghum. We were really hungry, so we couldn't begin to believe something so fairytale-like, that a time will ever come when "you'll be able to eat your fill."

I remember other things, too. Mother's younger brother was ordered to take part in the attack on Pearl Harbor, in a submarine leaving from Kure Naval Base near Hiroshima. Looking severe, wearing his military sword with its white haft, he came to say his final farewell. I remember the occasion. Father kept him here so long he almost missed curfew. Father pleaded with him: "Don't die! If you die in this war, your death will serve no purpose." My uncle was a model gung-ho officer; he would have died happily for the emperor. After having had to listen to Father's proselytizing, he left Kure on a submarine bound for Pearl Harbor. However, shortly before the submarine got to Pearl Harbor, it ran aground in the mud of the sea floor. The oxygen inside the submarine started to give out, and the crew were sure they were all about to die. My uncle was chief engineer. He tried desperately to reverse the engines and with the last of the fuel, finally pulled free of the ocean floor. By the time they floated free, the attack on Pearl Harbor was already over. When he didn't return, Mom grieved, thinking her younger brother was dead.

After a couple of days, the submarine returned to Kure. We were glad to learn he was alive. After the war ended, he was discharged from the navy and visited us. He said with feeling, "I had been proselytized by my brother-in-law, and when we sailed for Pearl Harbor, I thought my heart would stop beating. At a time when I thought I would have died happily for the emperor, I was really surprised to hear, 'Down with the emperor system!' And I sailed after having been admonished that Japan will lose. But that's what happened. It turned out exactly as he predicted." Father was stubborn through and through. We too heard similar lectures constantly. I remember vaguely that a year before I went to elementary school, Father said to us, "It's because of the emperor system that we can't eat. We are suffering like this because of the emperor system."

1944 passed, and in April and May of 1945, Hiroshima experienced air-raid alarms almost daily. In July, these alarms grew more frequent. Battleship *Yamato* lay at anchor at Kure, and day after day B-29s passed over Hiroshima to drop fire-bombs on Kure. Consequently, when we looked up at night in the direction of Kure, the sky was bright red from the fires. And when we looked to the west, toward Iwakuni, Kudamatsu, Tokuyama and their many munitions factories, the sky was also bright red.

The air-raid sirens sounded, but no attack came. Once in a while a formation of three carrier planes attacked the city, fired machine guns—rat-a-tat—and then flew off. I remember that one of the bullets landed in the alley behind our house, but it caused almost no damage. Under such circumstances, people in Hiroshima became wholly used to the situation. Some guy in the neighborhood said, with much show of truth, "I listened to a shortwave transmission from the U.S. military. They won't attack Hiroshima because they plan to turn it into a base." So people came to believe it firmly: "Hiroshima is safe." When B-29s flew over and the air-raid alarms sounded while we kids and our friends were playing, we'd routinely take cover in a bomb shelter to avoid the risk of bombing, but everyone in the bomb shelter believed it was only observation planes that would fly off soon.

It was a carefully calculated plan. For six months before dropping the atomic bomb, the U.S. forces had conditioned the people of Hiroshima to think we were safe.

Then came August 6th, the day of the atomic bombing.

2. WHERE I WAS ON AUGUST 6 WHEN THE BOMB EXPLODED

At about 7:15 a.m. on August 6, the first air-raid siren sounded. We didn't remember sirens sounding that early in the morning. However, they said there was danger, so we all took refuge in the shelter in front of our house. I thought it was probably an observation plane, and sure enough, the B-29 soon veered, and the alarm was lifted. We felt safe—it was simply a reconnaissance flight—and trooped out of the shelter.

The American army had been waiting for that precise moment. In those days, there were about 400,000 people in Hiroshima. Had they dropped the atomic bomb while the alert was in effect, about two-thirds of the people in Hiroshima would have been in bomb shelters and would have survived. They intentionally had the B-29 turn off to make everyone feel safe and disperse. That was the situation they created: 400,000 people all started their morning routines.

This is what my family was doing. Mother, pregnant, was hanging out the laundry on the clothes-drying porch off the second floor. At that time, there was no summer vacation, so we had to go to school, and when I went to the entryway, Eiko, my elder sister, a sixth-grader, was in the nine-by-twelve room next to the entryway. She said, "You go on ahead. I'll come after I get my school things organized." She was arranging her school things on the table. Beside the entryway was a nine-by-nine room, and Father was reading the newspaper and thinking about setting to work. My younger brother Susumu, four years old, was plumped down in the entryway, holding a model warship and singing: "Tater, tater, white potato, sweet potato." Leaving them there, I set out with the neighborhood kids for school.

Kanzaki Elementary School was less than a mile from our house. The school fronted on the trolley street linking the town of Eba, just to the south, and Yokogawa, a suburb on the northern edge of the city. Quite wide, the street still exists today. Kanzaki Elementary School fronted on the street and was surrounded by a concrete wall that formed a big U. We crossed the ditch along the street and entered through the gate. All the neighborhood kids went in. Inside the gate was the schoolyard, without protection of any kind; so had I entered the gate together with my friends, I wouldn't have survived.

Life or death? A person's fate is truly a matter of mere chance. I too was on the point of entering the gate. But a moment before I did, I was stopped by a classmate's mother who came chasing after me. She asked, "The air-raid alert sounded a while ago. Are today's classes at the school or at the temple?" Back then, because of the danger of bombing, those in the lower grades went on alternate days to the school and a local temple. I replied, "I don't know yet." I talked with my back leaning against the wall.

THE ENOLA GAY TOOK OFF FROM TINIAN BASE AT 2:45 A.M., FOLLOWED BY TWO OBSERVATION PLANES.

THE DROPPING OF THE BOMB WAS SCHEDULED FOR 9:15 A.M. (8:15 A.M. JAPAN TIME), AUGUST 6...

VA-ROOOMM

I happened to look up. The sky of Hiroshima on August 6th was bright blue, cloudless. Into that bright blue sky, suddenly, came a B-29, its vapor trail stretching out behind. Ahead of the vapor trail the duraluminum body glittered in the sunlight. Seeing the plane, I told her: "Ma'am, it's a B-29." She looked up and said, "Yes, a B-29."

However, the air-raid alerts did not sound as they had earlier that morning. Only a short while before, when the enemy plane appeared, the air-raid alerts had sounded just before it appeared in the sky. However, this *Enola Gay*, the plane carrying the atomic bomb, flew into the skies above Hiroshima, and no air-raid alarms sounded.

For me it remains a mystery to this day. Why didn't the air-raid alarms sound? I can't help wondering whether the fix might have been in.

Soon after the plane passed overhead and its vapor trail faded, the atomic bomb exploded.

11

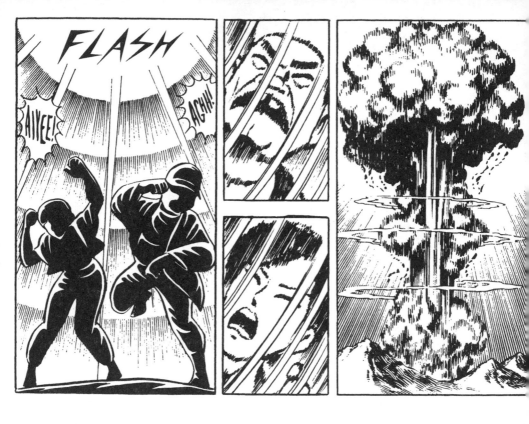

Even now, I can close my eyes and see the colors of the atomic bomb the moment it exploded. A pale light, like phosphorus burning furiously, white at its center, a great ball of light with yellow and red mixing at its edges. This enormous ball of fire seared itself onto my retinas. The moment I saw the light, I lost consciousness. When I came to, it was pitch dark. Broad daylight had become pitch dark. I raised my head, "Can it be night?" A six-inch nail, protruding from a board, had struck me; the scar remains on my right cheek to this day. I made to stand up, the skin tore, and blood ran down my cheek.

Frightened to death in this bizarre situation, I wiped away what I thought was sweat but was actually blood. When I tried to stand up, I discovered that roof tiles, bricks, scraps of lumber lay on top of me. The concrete wall, too, had fallen over and was covering me. Frantically, I pushed at the roof tiles and wood on top of me and scrambled my way out; when I looked in front, the mother of my classmate had been blown into the center of the trolley street. Her body had been burned pitch-black all over. Her clothing was gone. Only fragments hung around her neck. At that time, women wore work pants, so some fragments of the work pants also remained, but the rest had been burned pitch-black. Her hair was in tatters; her white eyes, wide open, glared at me.

It was truly a miracle that I survived. When the atomic bomb exploded, the center was millions of degrees hot. The rays that hit people on the ground were 5,000 to 6,000 degrees hot. Horrendous heat rays —they could melt iron instantly— covered all of Hiroshima. Everyone above ground was burned instantaneously. The concrete wall of the elementary school shielded me from the heat rays and allowed me to survive. The flash merely touched the back of my head from behind. Even now, I have two keloid scars on the back of my neck and head, and there's a bald

IN HIRO-SHIMA, TIME STOPPED...

GROAN...

W-WHA-? WHAT HAPPENED? IT'S PITCH DARK!

IS IT NIGHT ALREADY? BUT I WAS ON MY WAY TO SCHOOL...!

W-WHY AM I UNDER THIS WALL?

SOMETHING FLASHED. AFTER THAT I DON'T REMEMBER A THING...

spot on the back of my head. Had I stepped just a bit away from the wall, I would have been burned pitch-black, just like the mother of my classmate. That concrete wall saved my life.

Moreover, a blast then hit the city, at 140 miles an hour, and all over Hiroshima buildings were knocked down and blown away. I, too, would have been blown away, along with the school wall. It was truly a miracle. Back then, large trees had been planted along the sidewalk that ran along the wall. The blast broke those trees off near the ground, leaving about two feet of trunk sticking up. The wall fell over onto those stumps, which propped up the wall at an angle, and I was saved from being crushed flat. So second and third miracles saved me. I was so shocked when I saw the mother of my classmate, burned pitch-black. Immediately I rushed out into the trolley street. There, for the first time, I grasped the reality of the situation. At the time, along the trolley line in Funairi Hommachi stood rows of two-story houses that belonged to old established families. All these houses had collapsed completely, as if razed. The second stories lay in a heap, undulating off into the distance; the first stories had collapsed completely, as if they had exploded. So it was clear that the extremely strong blast had come from directly above. I looked at the scene with stunned eyes, wondering what had happened. Drop India ink into water, and it thins and spreads. In just that way smoke covered Hiroshima.

3. THE PROCESSION OF GHOSTS

What goes through people's minds at such a time? Thrust suddenly into extremity, they are reduced to instinct. They think only of going home. People think of nothing else. As if in a dream, my feet moved toward home. I went along the trolley street as the pale smoke drifted, and the first people I met were five or six women wearing only loose shirts. Hiroshima's summers are very hot, so that's all they'd been wearing. I approached them and saw they had countless pieces of glass sticking into their flesh: some of the women on the left, others on the right, some of the women in the front, still others on the back. It depended entirely on their location relative to the nearest window. Those who had had windows on their left had glass splinters only on their left side. From the top of their head to their shoulders, only their left side was covered with glass. And those who'd been facing windows had their fronts covered with glass. Some had glass only on their right; others, only on their back. How could glass pierce the human body that way? I was amazed.

They were bleeding. One woman, the shoulder strap of her chemise cut, had her breast exposed. Her breast and pale skin were blue. I stared at her, wondering why the blue color, and I found that the edges of the glass were blue. Her body looked blue

THEY WALKED ALONG, DRIPPING BLOOD.

because she was covered with blue-edged glass. When she moved her arms and legs, the glass jingled.

More and more aghast, I made my way as if in a dream and found on the sidewalk along the other side of the street naked people burned so black I couldn't tell male from female. They sat with legs outstretched. As if they were simpletons, their eyes were wide open, fixed on a point in the sky; they showed no sign of volition.

At the time, cisterns holding water to fight fires had been installed at fixed intervals along the right-hand sidewalk. Un-injured people scooped up water from these cisterns. Those sitting on the street, burned black, and those whose bodies were full of glass noticed the water and crawled to these cisterns. To wash off the blood, women with innumerable glass splinters scooped up water with their hands and poured it all over themselves.

To avoid cutting their fingers on the glass when they touched it with their bare hands, they picked up rags to pull out the glass. And those who were burned black took the water and drank it. The burns made them thirsty.

They clustered around the cisterns. In scenes of carnage in movies or on the stage, voices cry, "Ouch!" "It's awful!" "Help!" But those scenes aren't real. In the real carnage of an extreme situation, people utter not a single word but are completely silent. As if you are watching a silent movie, you hear not a single word. There were only movements: people simply pulled out glass because it hurt, simply drank water by scooping it up in their hands. They never expressed will or feelings—not at all.

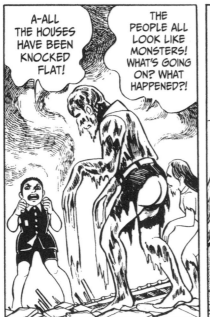

Note: These panels are from the author's graphic novel "Barefoot Gen" in which Susumu's name has been changed to Shinji, and the author's name changed to Gen.

I grew more and more agitated, more and more desperate, and ran along the trolley line until finally I reached the alley leading to our house. I ran down it. The houses on both sides of the alley were on fire, and I couldn't get close to our house.

Flames are truly frightening. Even though the passageway was fairly wide, flames crept along the ground. The flames reached out from both sides, as if joining hands, and in an instant the road became a sea of fire. The alley functioned like a chimney.

A horrible hot wind blew along it. So I felt instinctively that I couldn't get home, that it was too dangerous, and returned to the trolley street. When I emerged again onto the trolley line, my emotions began to kick in, seemingly for the first time. Anxiety seized me: my family has abandoned me, I'm all alone. This time I ran back and forth on the trolley line, searching for my family, crying desperately, "Daddy! Mommy!" The street was the cruelest scene imaginable. People were crawling along whose bellies had been ripped open by the pressure of the blast; they dragged their intestines. People whose eyes were blown out by the blast: their eyeballs hung down onto their cheeks. People burnt black were wandering back and forth. They formed a teeming mass.

I searched for Mother, crying, "Mommy! Mommy!" Luckily the woman from next door found me. She too had glass all over her body; she was bleeding profusely. She told me, "Just before Eba on this trolley line, there's a stop called Funairi Kawaguchi. Your mother's there. Go!" So I headed frantically for Eba.

However, I couldn't run. The crowd escaping in the direction of Eba was walking very slowly. They'd been struck by rays as hot as 11,000 degrees, so their skin immediately blistered up. Blisters—some as big as six inches—covered their bodies. When they walked, the fluid inside the blisters sloshed. When due to some jolt the blisters burst, the liquid poured out, and the skin peeled off. The skin over their chests peeled off, from the shoulders down; the backs of their hands peeled. The skin of their arms peeled away, down to the five fingernails. So skin a yard long dangled from the fingertips of both hands. The skin on backs peeled off, down to the waist. So it hung like a loose loincloth. The skin of legs peeled off, down to the ankles. All the people looked like ghosts. If they walked with their arms down, the skin hanging off their fingertips dragged on the ground. That was painful, so they raised their hands. They appeared ghost-like. And the skin of their legs, dragging along on the ground, prevented them from running. So they shuffled along, a step at a time, the skin of their legs dragging along the ground.

I noticed a strange thing in this sluggish procession. Some had had dark clothes on: their clothes were consumed completely, down to the last thread. Others had had on white shirts or white short-sleeved shirts or white pants: some of that white clothing was completely intact. Why was white the only clothing that remained intact? The white clothing had acted as a mirror, sending the heat rays bouncing back. Black clothing had absorbed them: both clothes and bodies had burned. Among this crowd, I walked along the trolley line.

4. I FIND MOTHER

I had made it to the Funairi Kawaguchi trolley stop, and on the sidewalk on the left sat Mother, in her apron, on a thin *futon* on the sidewalk, some pots alongside, her face sooty, her expression vacant.

I had finally found her, and relief came. I sank to the ground beside her. Neither of us had the energy to say a thing. I looked carefully: Mom was holding something wrapped in a blanket. When I peeked inside, it was a baby. The shock of the disaster had sent Mother into labor, and she had given birth on the pavement to a baby girl. Thus, on that August 6th, my sister was born. We named her Tomoko, but she died four months later. Was it malnutrition? The effects of radiation? I'm not sure.

That's how I found Mother, and I squatted, dazed, on the pavement. I watched the procession of ghosts continuing from the direction of downtown. They shuffled, dragging skin from both legs, so dust swirled into the air. This procession of ghosts passed, one after another, before me. One after another, people with skin hanging from fingers passed before me.

At Funairi Kawaguchi, the trolley went up and over a low rise. On both sides of the rise the fields were lower; they were used to grow sweet potatoes and vegetables. When people got there, they tumbled down into these vegetable fields on either side of the trolley line. They lay directly on top of the plants. Seared by the rays, their entire bodies must have been hot and painful. When they fell onto the plants, the cool of the plants against their skin must have felt good. So they lay on top of the plants. As I watched, the vegetable fields on either side of the trolley line turned into row upon row of people with burnt skin.

All Hiroshima was without power, and there were no electric lights at all, but the region was going up in flames, a waterfall flowing upward, and by the light of flames, you could see clearly even at night. I felt very sleepy and dozed but I couldn't sleep. I heard something that sounded as if dozens of insects had flown into my ear. As evening deepened into night the sound persisted and grew, and I opened my eyes. It turned out to be a chorus of one word: "Water!" "Water!" "Water!" That was the only word. Just "Water!" "Water!" Mother said, "Go and scoop up some water!" I picked up a metal helmet that was rolling about on the pavement, went to a cistern and scooped water again and again. Mother found a broken teacup, scooped water from the helmet, and offered it to a person right beside her who was groaning, "Water!" "Water!" When, carrying the teacup, she approached him, he seemed to catch the scent of water, bent over the cup, and emptied it in one gulp. Three or four seconds

after he gulped the water, he collapsed, and his head struck the ground. We offered water to the next person, and he died, and his head struck the ground. One after another, they drank and died.

So a rumor spread quickly: "Under no circumstances give water to people with burns. Give them water, and they'll die." No matter how desperately they wanted it, we were told not to give them any. It was really a strange phenomenon: one after another, they died as soon as we gave them water. Unable to crawl by themselves to the cistern, they seemed driven by instinct to drink water because of the burns over their entire bodies. With "Water!" as their sole thought, they clung to life. When we gave them water, they died of shock.

5. CORPSES, MAGGOTS, FLIES

August 7. The sun was glaring down on Hiroshima. In the potato and vegetable fields almost everyone was dead. The procession of ghosts from the center of the city was much larger than on the previous day, and their numbers continued to grow. Now there was no space for newcomers to collapse onto. I wondered what they'd do. People pulled the corpses, by hand or foot, to the edges of the fields. In the corners, piles arose of corpses of burned people. The next ghostlike people to arrive collapsed in the spaces that had opened up in the field. In the August heat corpses rotted immediately; they gave off the eerie stench of death. The strong smell made us vomit, but there was nothing we could do.

Beginning the seventh or eighth of August, an army battalion stationed in nearby Hiroshima, civilian wardens, relief squads and organizations of women came to offer aid.

We spent one week on that sidewalk. My oldest brother, a student who'd been mobilized, was working at Kure Naval Arsenal. We stayed there on the sidewalk until he came back so he would know we'd survived. However, we were surrounded with a sort of trade-show display of horrendous corpses of all kinds; the stench of death was suffocating. I found an umbrella, opened it out over the baby, and held it. But not able to stand the heat, I consulted with Mother, and we agreed to go and look for shade; carrying the baby, we started walking toward Eba, the end of the trolley line.

We headed for a place that had become an army firing range. It was a broad field, behind which was a low hill, Sarayama. We climbed the hill hoping to find shade under its big trees.

However, when we climbed the hill, almost all the big trees had at their base burn victims who had fled from the city; all the way to the top of the hill all the trees were taken. So we couldn't find shade. Three days after the bombing, we saw people whose burns were rotting, oozing pus and infested with maggots. Enormous numbers of maggots were wriggling. Maggots infest wounds very quickly. Their eggs are airborne and attach to the pus; with plenty to feed on, they turned into maggots with frightening speed. It must be impossibly painful and itchy. So everyone was using twigs for chopsticks and picking the maggots off their bodies in silence. All the way up the hill, these people encircled the big trees; we couldn't find shade, so we turned back.

An army relief tent had been set up at the base of the hill. By this time, I too was hurting from the burns on the back of my head, which prickled and from which pus was flowing. I went to the relief tent hoping to get treated with mercurochrome, but they looked at me as if to say, Why ever did you come here? They had no medicine, not even mercurochrome. The tent was surrounded by people seeking treatment for their burns. I returned to the tent a while later, and some of the people waiting there were already dead, and lots of corpses lay around.

Human beings are really amazing: no matter how horrible it was being surrounded with corpses, we adapted quickly to our environment. I stepped over the corpses of burned people, unfeeling. The rotten skin of the corpses peeled off; like banana skins, it clung to the soles of my feet. Even as I stepped on those corpses, I felt nothing at all. It was as if they were pieces of lumber. It is terrible that our human emotions atrophy so readily.

We returned to the place where we'd stayed before and waited for my older brother to return. No trains were running, so he walked all the way back to Hiroshima from Kure. The Hiroshima to which he came back was a wasteland—nothing at all as far as the eye could see. He got to where our house had been, resigned to the probability that his entire family had been killed. Neighbors were cremating relatives. They told him Mother and I were alive, and finally he managed to find us.

Then the four of us—Mother, brother, I, and the baby—moved in with an acquaintance in Eba, a town where some people farmed and some fished. Counting the baby, four of us barged in. Food was extremely scarce, so people resented our presence. We had nothing other than a blanket, pots and the kettle Mother had picked up on the sidewalk; we had nowhere else to go. Mother pleaded with them to allow us to stay, and we secured a shed-like room nine feet by twelve.

6. THE DEATHS OF FATHER, SISTER, BROTHER

Having found sanctuary, Mother regained some peace of mind, some normality. I asked her what had happened to Father and elder sister and younger brother, and for the first time Mother spoke in detail. Mother had survived the atomic bomb quite miraculously.

I knew that Mother had been hanging up clothes on the porch off the second floor. Mother finished hanging up the clothes and went to enter the house and had just moved under the overhang of the eaves. Old Japanese houses had very broad eaves. The atomic bomb exploded at the precise moment she stepped under the overhang. The single layer of wood that formed the eaves blocked the violent rays. Had she not been under it, her whole body would have been burned black. Had she gone a step further into the house, she would have been crushed at once. She survived because she was under the eaves. The blast levelled the house itself, but the drying porch floated up into the air. The moment the house collapsed, the drying porch flew up into the air carrying Mother, and she floated down to earth safely. Huge belly and all, Mother survived miraculously, without even a scratch. At the time, there were about 400,000 people living in Hiroshima. So some did survive, each in uniquely miraculous ways. Mother and I were among them.

Seven rivers flow through Hiroshima. So rivers were close. If we wanted to swim, we had our choice of places. On their way to school that day, some grade-school pupils decided to play hooky and go swimming instead. They took off their clothes and went in. Their teacher came walking along the river-bank. Getting caught was a big deal, so all of them dived under the water so the teacher wouldn't see them. When they surfaced out of breath, the teacher was dead, and the whole city was destroyed. Many people survived in such ways. It was a miracle. Had the teacher never come walking by at that time, they would have been swimming nonchalantly and been burned over their whole bodies.

When Mother came to herself after she was blown off the porch and down onto the road, from the direction of the entryway she heard my younger brother Susumu crying. She rushed to the entryway, and Susumu, his head pinned to the threshold by rafters, was pounding his feet on the floor and crying, "Mommy! Ouch! Ouch!" Susumu had been sitting in the entryway playing with model ships, so when the house collapsed, thick rafters pinned his head to the threshold. From the next room, demolished, Mother heard Father's voice, scolding, "Quick! Do something!" She heard no sound from Eiko who was in the nine-by-twelve room. Eiko must have died instantly. Mother pulled at everything— roof tiles, timbers, red clay—and tried everything to lift the rafters. But old houses had heavy rafters, and they fell on top of each other, so she couldn't free Susumu. She tried everything but got nowhere. So Mother appealed desperately to people fleeing along the road, "Please lend a hand! Please help me lift the rafters!" People tried two or three times, but they wouldn't move. Then they said, "It's no use!" and ran off.

It's quite natural. In such a scene of carnage, people are preoccupied with their own problems. They have no time or energy to take care of others.

In time, the flames gradually neared our house. Desperate to save at least Susumu, Mother inserted a piece of lumber between the rafters pinning him down to try to pry up the roof, but they wouldn't move. She couldn't lift them at all. The flames were approaching. Utterly lost, Mom sat by Susumu, crying, and when she put her arm around him, Susumu moved sideways. He moved, but his head didn't come free. Susumu cried, "Mommy!

Ouch! Ouch!" The flames were nearer. Half-crazed, Mother squatted in the entryway next to Susumu, crying, "Mommy will die with you! I'll die with all of you!" The flames were spreading. A neighbor who lived behind us came running past our house and saw Mother. When he saw her, he told her, "Nakazawa-san, there's no point in your dying, too! For them it's too late!" Prying Mother's hands from the entryway of our house, he got her to flee the flames.

Mother underwent two years of treatment in the Atomic Bomb Hospital and two years at home—in all, four years of illness. She died in 1966. Until her dying breath, she kept explaining to us how the flames had attacked our house and how it had become a pillar of fire and how as she escaped she had heard the voices of Susumu and Father out of the flames. The voice of Susumu: "Mommy! It's hot." "Hot!" Father's reproaches coming out of the flames, "Kimiyo! Can't you do something?" Mother always complained to us, "I can't get their voices out of my head." Her guilt at not being able to rescue them kept torturing her.

That's how Father, sister, brother died, so Mother directed us: "Go to the ruins of our house and retrieve their bones." So my brother and I took shovel and bucket and went to the entryway of our home. The earth was too hot to stand on for long. Jumping from one foot to the other, we stood at the entrance and looked around. Father was a Japanese-style painter, so he had dozens of ceramic paint pots. Many of them were scattered about, melted, fused, and twisted. There was no doubt these ruins had been our house.

We began to dig in the entryway. We found the skull of a small child, as expected. The skull of a small child is pure white, beautiful. Then we found more bones. I remember vividly—with my whole body—the moment I held his skull. The August sun was still strong, and it was stiflingly hot, yet when I held his skull, a chill came over me as if someone had dumped a bucket of ice on my back. "How hot he must have been! His head pinned, his feet beating on the floor." Today there are new building materials and in case of fire, we may be killed by toxic gas from those materials, suffocated within two or three breaths. In a way, it might be an easier death. But at the time there were no such materials.

With his head pinned by the beams, he was conscious as the flames ate at his body. Father too: he burned to death slowly, still conscious. I can't imagine a crueler way of killing. If they're going to kill us, they should kill us in less painful ways.

Then we dug in the room next to the entrance and found Father's skull and bones. We dug in the nine-by-twelve room and found the bones of my sister Eiko. We wanted to believe that these were bones of some outsiders who just happened to be in our house, that Father, sister, and brother managed to escape, but we found the bones exactly where Mother had told us to look, so we had to believe they'd died there. As we transferred the skulls and parts of bones to the bucket, we were covered all over with dust.

7. MOTHERS SHIELDING CHILDREN, BROTHERS SHIELDING SISTERS

Older people know well that during the war, concrete cisterns—three feet by three feet—filled with water stood at every entryway, for use against fires started by bombs. Those concrete cisterns were the only things still standing in the burnt-out waste of Hiroshima. Cisterns beyond count were visible all over. I approached a cistern thinking to use its water to wash the dirt off my hands and legs. I found that all the cisterns held half-burned, reddened corpses. I looked at these corpses closely: even in their final moments, they died deaths that attested to their human feelings at the last. Mothers died, wrapping their children in a tight embrace.

THIS WOMAN WAS TRYING TO SAVE HER CHILDREN BY HOLDING THEM TIGHT. BUT ALL IN VAIN...

FIRE CISTERN

When people in the river died of burns, faces swelled as big as soccer balls; arms swelled as much as eight inches thick, and bodies swelled to three times their normal size. The embrace of this mother was so tight that the child's face, swollen, was engulfed in the mother's body. The way she died showed her maternal instincts and commitment to protect her children, as much as possible. from the heat of the fire. In the next cistern were an elder brother and a younger sister. The brother died a brotherly death, protecting his sister. He was on top of his sister to protect her as much as possible—a brotherly concern. And brother and sister, holding each other close, had died in the cistern. Almost all the cisterns held such bodies. So the atomic bomb instantly incinerated everyone who was outdoors, and its blast crushed people in their houses. Those who managed to survive the first moments were encircled with fire; the flames surrounding them and incinerating them, too. Unable to endure the heat, they had jumped into the cisterns. We walked toward the center of the city, into the western business district, an area called Dobashi. Dobashi was a glamorous part of town, with a red-light district and movie theaters. A small cistern contained more than thirty corpses piled on top of each other. Surrounded by flames and unable to bear the heat, people had jumped in. The stench of death was enough to make us faint.

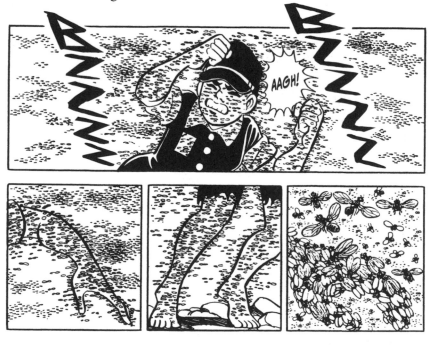

Moreover, as if myriad pebbles were being hurled against my body, flies started attacking me. I couldn't even open my eyes; flies flew into my mouth and ears. Because it was downtown, many corpses were piled up, and all these flies had bred on the corpses. Squinting, I saw that the flies turned white clothing black instantaneously. So when we went downtown, we had to keep a towel in each hand and whip them about. Even now, I still feel afraid of flies whenever I see them. I am terrified they might eat me alive.

After passing through Dobashi, we came to Tōkaichi. We turned right at Tōkaichi, and there was Sakan, then Aioibashi, the bridge located adjacent to the Atomic Bomb Dome. You may know it well from photographs. The river Aioibashi spans is the Honkawa river, the river that flows through the center of Hiroshima.

When we looked down from the bridge, the river was filled completely with masses of corpses, burned and swollen. They floated back and forth, upstream with high tide, downstream toward the mouth of the river at ebb. The intestines of the corpses were rotting, and gas built up in their stomachs, giving them large pot bellies. Swollen bellies popped from that pressure, and water poured in. The corpses grew heavy and sank to the bottom. All the seven rivers in Hiroshima were filled with corpses. There were tremendous numbers of corpses.

People say that in Hiroshima somewhere from one hundred to two hundred thousand people were killed by the atomic bomb, but to this day there is no exact count.

Many of the corpses were piled onto trucks and brought to the Army firing range in Eba. At first, they lined the corpses up neatly and cremated them. However, so many corpses were brought to the site that there were just too many for such care, so the soldiers put the corpses in huge piles, poured fuel oil over them, and set them ablaze. So at the broad firing range, the oil cremating the corpses sent up columns of smoke. The fires burned night and day for almost two months after the defeat. Skulls were piled in a dozen piles nearly six feet tall. They were left exposed to the elements for some six months. Soon after Japan surrendered, the U.S. Army landed and found the piles of skulls left out in the open. Even those guys probably felt ashamed. They brought in bulldozers, covered the bones with dirt, crushed them, and buried them. Today's Eba Junior High School stands on that site. Dig in the schoolyard of the junior high, and even now you'll turn up skulls. I know because I saw it all. Such enormous numbers of corpses were cremated. They were cremated not only in Eba, but almost everywhere in Hiroshima, too.

8. AFTER THE SURRENDER

It was at Eba on August 15th that we learned that Japan had lost the war. However, we couldn't give any thought at all to that development. All we thought about was how to survive. Eba— half-farming, half-fishing—was a closed community, and people who came from elsewhere were viewed with hostility: "Outsider! Outsider!" The people were set in their parochialism and bullied us: "Here come the outsiders!" A gang of young thugs used to attack me. Just for the fun of it, they hit me on the back of my head where the burn had finally scabbed over. The scab broke, and blood and pus oozed. I was really mortified. One on one, I'd never have lost, but they attacked in a group—"Outsider! Outsider!" Mother, too: she was accused of stealing an umbrella and lying about it, surrounded by people, dragged to the nearby police sub-station, falsely accused, and forced to sign a letter of apology.

Today Japanese talk a lot about democracy, love and peace, but I feel I saw the true nature of the Japanese people. In extreme situations, humans behave with extreme cruelty. That's how bad we had it.

However, you have to go on. How to survive? They wouldn't share their food. We had to provide for ourselves. Fortunately, Eba had its shoreline, and when the tide ebbed, we worked hard digging clams and gathering seaweed; because there was no salt, we also scooped up seawater. The clams and seaweed and the wild grass and weeds that we gathered along the roadside: we put it all into the brine and boiled it. We tasted things to see if they were edible and managed to survive eating clams and broth. The human desire to survive is incredibly powerful. The proof? I am alive today. But then we were so starved that it might have driven us crazy. Actually, we were so hungry we felt faint.

We fought desperately to find food. At last, because of all the bullying, we fled from Eba and built a hut at Takajō, right next to the Atomic Bomb Dome, and our postwar life began. I transferred to Honkawa Elementary School, a three-story concrete building located on the riverbank opposite the Dome and received a postwar education.

However, all the ceilings of the building had collapsed, so it was nothing like a school. When it rained, we rushed to the corners of the classroom for shelter. In the winter, snowflakes danced in the classroom. There was nothing: no blackboards, no desks, no podium. Such was our school. Occasionally, depending on the direction of the wind, we could smell the stench of death in the classroom because there were a lot of bodies buried nearby. Under such conditions, all we did at school was physical ed. I simply don't remember learning anything. After school I cultivated the wasteland to grow potatoes, vegetables, food of all kinds.

My turf was the area at the base of the Dome. In summer, we dove off Aioi Bridge into the Honkawa. When you dove into the river and swam along the bottom, you saw many, many skulls. On both banks of the river: skulls. A horrendous number of human bones. Dig in the river below the Dome even today, and you'll turn up plenty of bones. In places where there were many bones, freshwater shrimp two inches long were particularly plentiful. So when the tide ebbed, I'd run a foot of thread through a needle and take a net to the spots where there were lots of bones. I'd catch shrimp and string them through the midsection. I'd collect shrimp until I had a full thread. They were protein for our family. The shrimp got fat feeding on the corpses, and we ate them, so it was really cannibalism; but such was our diet at the time.

9. THE ATOMIC BOMB ORPHANS

The tragedy did not end there. In the atomic wasteland there were some 6,000 atomic bomb orphans. Those who were honest and meek and not given to committing crimes gathered in front of Hiroshima Station, where lots of people came and went. To keep warm in winter, the orphans burned wood in large metal drums and slept in a circle around the drums. They all suffered from malnutrition. They barely opened their eyes when passers-by walked past. Even if they opened their eyes, they hadn't the energy to get to their feet. The next day several of them would already be dead, and others would have taken their places. These orphans were merely awaiting death from malnutrition. If they wanted to survive in such circumstances, they either banded together to commit theft or became lone-wolf thieves. So Hiroshima led the nation in juvenile crime. I believe that what they did was natural, not all that bad. How else could they survive?

Seven years had passed after the atomic bombing before a helping hand was offered the orphans. Seven years after the bombing, a movement to help them began at last. Up to that time, no one had offered them a hand. If Mother had died, I too would have been orphaned and become one of them. Had I taken one wrong step, I might have become a gangster, committed murder, died a beggar. They had two choices: either die of mal-nutrition or survive by turning criminal.

Fierce gangster wars took place in Hiroshima. The gangs said to the orphans, "Kill one of the enemy leaders, and we'll take care of you." So they used the orphans as hit men. The orphans were expendable. They had no parents, no relatives, and no one complained when they were killed. In seven years kids who had been sixth graders at the time of the atomic bomb had already become young men. I knew children who lived a comfortable life before the war who were orphaned and used by gangs and died as hit men. Left without family or relatives, they had no choice but to join a gang or to become career thieves. In this way, the crime that was the war did not stop in 1945; it continues to this day.

And then there's the matter of the secondary effects of radiation. In the month after the atomic bomb, people who had been healthy began dying, one after another. An uncle, Mother's younger brother, was in an army battalion stationed in Hiroshima. About five feet nine, he was ordered to clear away the corpses;

a couple of days later he paid a visit to our house and said, "Our job is to cart off the corpses." He went back to his post. Two or three days after that, someone from the army came to our hut and told Mother, "Your brother has died." Mother asked what happened to him—he had been so very alive only days earlier that she was stunned.

Because it was located far enough from the epicenter, Eba had not suffered great damage—just broken windows. But people from there who had searched in the ruins of Hiroshima to see if relatives were safe died within a week.

At the time, we knew nothing at all about radiation or atomic bombs. People called the bomb *Pikadon* or the "flash-boom" because there was a bright flash (*pika*) and then a boom (*don*), and the rumor was rampant that if you breathed the poisonous gas of the flash-boom, you'd be infected. The effects of radiation kicked in suddenly. At the moment the bomb exploded, it scattered radiation into the air, then lifted dust into the air to form a cloud. This cloud moved with the wind and dropped "black rain." Due to the radiation, those who got covered in black rain started to die rapidly, and residual radio-activity accumulated in the soil with that black rain. People who set foot there died strange deaths one after another, due to radiation disease. Now we know that this was the effect of secondary radiation.

The effects of radiation are really horrendous. The destructive power of nuclear weapons is also intense, but the residual radiation continues to kill the survivors. Thirty-seven years after the war, the number of victims of the bomb who have manifested symptoms of once-latent leukemias or cancers is increasing rapidly. How long will the effects of the atomic bomb continue? Even after all of us have died, there may be no final tally. The real terror of radiation is that it continues for decades to eat away at the bodies of the survivors.

10. I BECOME A CARTOONIST

That is the Hiroshima I lived in for twenty-two years. When I think of the pleasures of that period, there is only my cartooning. Beginning when I was a sixth-grader, I was devoted to cartoons and drew cartoons every day; when I entered junior high, I drew cartoons on postcards and mailed them to publishers in Tokyo, and they appeared occasionally in the "Contributions from Our Readers" column or got an honorable mention. By the time I graduated from junior high, I was really hooked, and I came to hope I could make a living as a cartoonist. At the time, it was very hard to find a job; I considered which occupations might lead to cartooning and chose sign painting. Sign painting would teach me the relationships among colors, design fundamentals, lettering. All these were essential foundations for cartoons. I spent my working days in the ruins of Hiroshima as a sign painter.

At the age of twenty-two, I made a break for Tokyo. For six months, I drafted trial pieces in my apartment and took my unsolicited manuscripts to publishers. Eventually, I was offered a serial for Boys' Illustrated Magazine and started life as a cartoonist. So my life as a cartoonist started auspiciously. From that time on, for the last twenty-two years, I have lived as a cartoonist.

At first, the thought of drawing cartoons about the atomic bomb never occurred to me. Every year, in Hiroshima, on August 6th, many, many people gather from all over Japan to attend a festival, the Hiroshima Peace Memorial Ceremony, commemorating the anniversary of the atomic bomb. The local papers report how many victims of Hiroshima have died that year at the atomic bomb hospital. Every time I saw those articles, I felt really uneasy. Whenever I saw "atomic bomb" in the newspaper, I didn't feel like reading the article; I was anxious, thinking that some day I would suffer the negative effects of radiation. When I went to bookshops and encountered a section for "Hiroshima" books where there was an array of books related to atomic bombs, I ducked past, eyes down. "I myself experienced it. So I'd like to keep my distance." Then I came to Tokyo and started my life as cartoonist.

However, when Mother died in 1966, I received a telegram, "MOTHER DEAD," and I returned immediately to Hiroshima. I came home and found my brother upset and grumbling. I asked him, "What's the matter?" He replied that immediately after Mother died, the Atomic Bomb Casualty Commission in Hiroshima sent someone to our house to insist that he donate Mother's organs. He chased them away: "You must be joking! You drop the atomic bomb upon us, and now you want to take Mother's body?"

As a matter of fact, the ABCC is a disaster. In the month after the atomic bomb, they came quickly to Hiroshima and, while there were still many bodies lying among the ruins, started collecting internal organs and other body parts. They collected pebbles as well. When I was in grade school, I saw a station wagon, with yellow and green stripes, coming and going daily. They had elementary school children bring in stool samples and then loaded the children in the wagon and drove off. The visits of the station wagon were strange. Why did they take so many children to the ABCC? I asked my teacher, "What are they doing?" She said, "I don't know." Later, I figured it out gradually. Honkawa Elementary School is located in the center of Hiroshima, so children who survived the atomic bomb came to it from a broad swath of the city. There could be no better guinea pigs. All the children who survived within a couple of miles of Ground Zero were attending the school. That's why they were taking these kids to their facility.

After the bombing, mother too frequently suffered health problems—anemia, stomach cramps, fainting spells. She had to go to clinics many times. The doctors said to her, "You should go to the ABCC. It's an American medical organization, and they'll provide you with good treatment. I'll refer you. Go there." So, like a drowning woman grasping at straws, Mother went to the ABCC. When she got there, she was stripped to the skin and told to put on a gown—a doubled sheet with a hole in the center

THEY STRIPPED MY MOTHER NAKED AND MADE HER WEAR A WHITE CLOTH...

...AND PEERED AT HER FROM ALL ANGLES, EXAMINING EVERY NOOK AND CRANNY OF HER BODY.

for her head. The gown hung down fore and aft. She made the rounds of the exam rooms and got examined from head to toe. After being examined, she received none of the results and no medicine. Mother grumbled, "Why ever did I go to that place and let my blood be drawn? I just made a fool of myself."

Doctors in Hiroshima referred victims of the nuclear bomb to the ABCC because in return they received the latest American medicines free of charge. Then they made money selling the medicines to other victims of the atomic bomb or to the general public. So they were eager to refer survivors to the ABCC. The ABCC collects all the data of survivors and never, ever, discloses the important parts of the data to the Japanese. Instead, they send the data to their lab in Washington D.C. to utilize it to prepare against possible nuclear war. They disclose only the unnecessary parts of the data to the Japanese.

The ABCC makes me very angry. The day after my mother's death, her body was cremated. I knew what cremated bones look like—I had seen so many bodies cremated in the ruins. The cremated remains of Mother were handed to me. I was surprised when I looked in the urn and saw no skull and no bones. There was only white powdery ash. I felt very angry because radiation had eaten away at Mother, to the marrow of her bones and not left even any bones. On the train back to Tokyo, I grew angry and disgusted. I tried to think through the war and the atomic bomb. I thought very hard. I arrived finally at the fact that we Japanese had not dealt with our responsibility for the war and with the atomic bomb.

The only thing I'm good at is cartoons. Hoping to appeal to the public through cartoons, I drew "Pelted by Black Rain," my first work on the atomic bomb, and then continued all the way to "Barefoot Gen," taking the war and the atomic bombs as main themes.

11. MY LIFE'S WORK: OPPOSING WAR AND THE ATOMIC BOMB

What annoyed me most was the thought that unlike other peoples, the Japanese people may take these things most lightly. A newsreel I saw in the ruins of Hiroshima still stands out in my mind. According to the newsreel, in Italy, they tied a rope around the legs of Mussolini's corpse, and citizens pulled it through the ruins. Then they threw the rope over a wooden frame, hoisted the body, and people—men, women, children, older people, young children—all stoned it. In their anger, thinking that he had put them in this utterly miserable situation, they stoned his corpse. Then they tore down the body and marched around the city. I watched the movie and was really impressed.

West Germany, too, was also quite different from Japan. They're still pursuing Nazi war criminals to the far corners of the earth to take them to court for war crimes. Their determination is really amazing.

And Japan? At the time of the defeat, unlike the Italians, the Japanese knelt on the ground in front of the Imperial Palace, crying, "Your Majesty, Japan has lost because we didn't work hard enough." Even in the post-war era, the emperor survives magisterially as "symbol," according to the constitution. A war criminal became prime minister even in the post-war era, with no qualms. The gang who actively promoted the war have everything their own way in the political and business establishment, comfortably, and still control politics. They set themselves up in comfort and order the people about. That's why people don't understand the cruelty of the war and the devastation of the atomic bombs.

Among the Japanese as a whole, awareness of responsibility for the war has faded. Some people profited from the war and insist on the necessity of rearmament or to fight wars to defend the country. For "merchants of death," there is no more profitable business than war.

I think it's still not too late. We have to overthrow these guys. The power of the current generation of nuclear weapons is incomparably greater than at the time of Hiroshima and Nagasaki. If two bombs explode, the whole of the Japanese archipelago will be destroyed: that's how horrible these weapons are.

Recently I watched a TV program where a critic insisted, "The Japanese should construct shelters to prepare against a nuclear war." It is no joke. If nuclear weapons are used, will there be time to get to a shelter? And even if you manage to get to a shelter, how will you survive when air, water, crops are all polluted with radiation? How many people can be accommodated in a shelter that can protect people for decades? The few who survive are sure to be high-ranking government officials. Even if shelters are built, ordinary people won't survive. They'll be annihilated. When critics talk plausibly about nuclear weapons on TV, I'm amazed to see people who don't understand nod matter-of-factly on hearing such nonsense. How little they understand!

They say Japan is the only nation to suffer atomic bombings, but I wonder if the Japanese are really aware of the actual consequences of nuclear bombs. You should know more about the real consequences before you talk: that's what I want to shout. Learning more isn't something you can leave to someone else to do. It's an issue each of us must tackle individually. It might happen to us all at any time. Nuclear disaster might be caused at any time not by nuclear war but by accident. There are reports in recent newspapers and broadcasts. There are accidents, such as a broken ventilator that almost caused a detonation, a small component costing only a few dollars that malfunctioned and nearly caused the accidental launch of an intercontinental ballistic missile. Then a B-52 on a practice mission carrying hydrogen bombs crashed on to the sea ice of Greenland. There was also an accident in which four out of five fail-safe devices failed. Nuclear explosion may happen at any time.

These issues can't be left to other people. The only way to tackle them is for each of us to fight desperately. The only thing I am good at is cartooning, so for the rest of my life I will keep dealing with the war and atomic bombs.

ABOUT THE
AUTHOR

Keiji Nakazawa was born in Hiroshima, and was six years old when the city was destroyed by an atomic bomb in 1945. All of his family members who had not been evacuated died in the bombing, except for his mother, and an infant sister who died several weeks after the bombing. Compelled to tell his story in the memory of his family, Keiji Nakazawa is best known for his epic tragic history Barefoot Gen. During his career, Nakazawa had over 50 book-length serials published in paperback format or in Japanese children's comic weeklies. Keiji Nakazawa retired from cartooning in 2009. He continued to lecture throughout Japan about the experience of atomic bomb victims, until his death in Hiroshima in 2012, at age 73. He is survived by his wife, daughter, and grandchildren.